imagine

A Book for BAND AID by DAVID BAILEY

Preface by WILLIAM GOLDING

THAMES AND HUDSON

FABER AND FABER

This edition © Copyright 1985 Band Aid
Photographs © Copyright 1985 David Bailey
Preface © Copyright 1985 William Golding

Text set by Foremost Typesetting Ltd, London
Monochrome origination by D. S. Colour International Ltd, London
Printed and bound in Great Britain by Balding + Mansell Ltd, Wisbech

Thanks to:

Valerie Blondeau of Band Aid

Bowater Corporation

Celloglas Ltd

D.S. Colour International Ltd

Matthew Evans of Faber and Faber

Foremost Typesetting Ltd

Philippe Garner of Sotheby's

William Golding

Iggesund Convertors

Kevin Jenden of Band Aid

Penny Jenden of Band Aid

Gerald Judd Ltd

Frank Lowe

Bill McAlister of the ICA

Thomas Neurath of Thames and Hudson

Adrian Paul

Nicola Redway of Sotheby's

Pete Townshend

. . . and to Balding + Mansell Ltd for printing and binding

Preface

When I was asked to write this preface I was sent a sheaf of the photographs which David Bailey has taken for the book. So I examined them all and I am not sure I shall ever be the same again. It is a clever and awful book, but this page is harmless and you can read it to the end without distress. If you are worldly-wise you will put the book down then. This is a warning. If you look further you will be caught. Most of the photographs are as harmless as this first page and that is the real cleverness of the book. For the pictures are up David Bailey's street and taken with the careful artistry you would expect from him – pictures of beautiful, glossy black people, sometimes in a state as near nature as possible. The book may well fall open at such a picture. It is a kind of Russian roulette. For here and there Bailey has slipped in quite another kind of journalist's pic: if the book opens at one of those, it will keep you awake tonight and perhaps make you feel you will stay awake for ever. We all know about the 'catastrophe' in Africa. But the word 'catastrophe' implies a load of statistics. It isn't emotive. A few of the photographs slipped into the book you are holding aren't about the 'catastrophe' at all. They are images of individual horror.

All the people concerned in this book have given their work without payment . . . they have seen the photographs and to do anything else would be unthinkable. This is not tragedy, for tragedy is a remembered thing. This is horror which goes on and on and on. So buy the book even if you don't look at the pictures. That's not much but it's something. The 'catastrophe' may be beyond human comprehension and beyond human capacity to remedy or prevent. But perhaps here and there the horror can be gentled a bit by your help.

And for the love of God and man be angry.

William Golding
May 1985

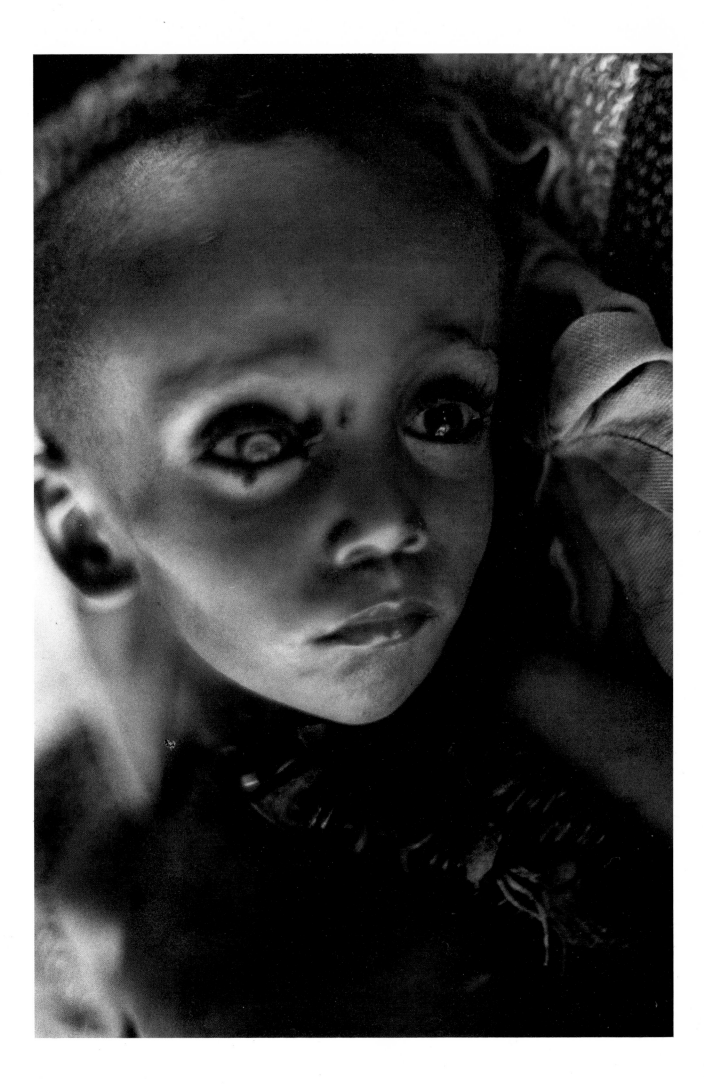

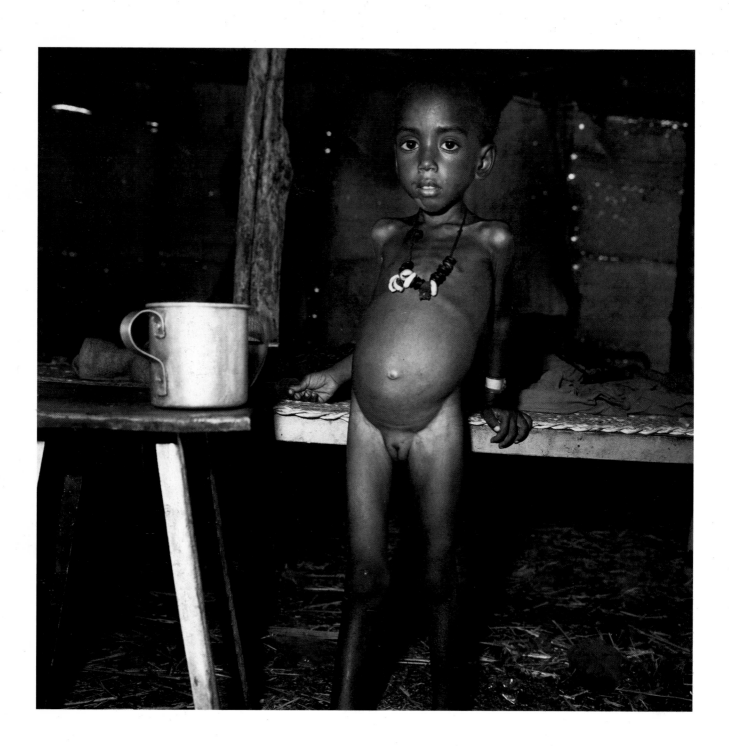

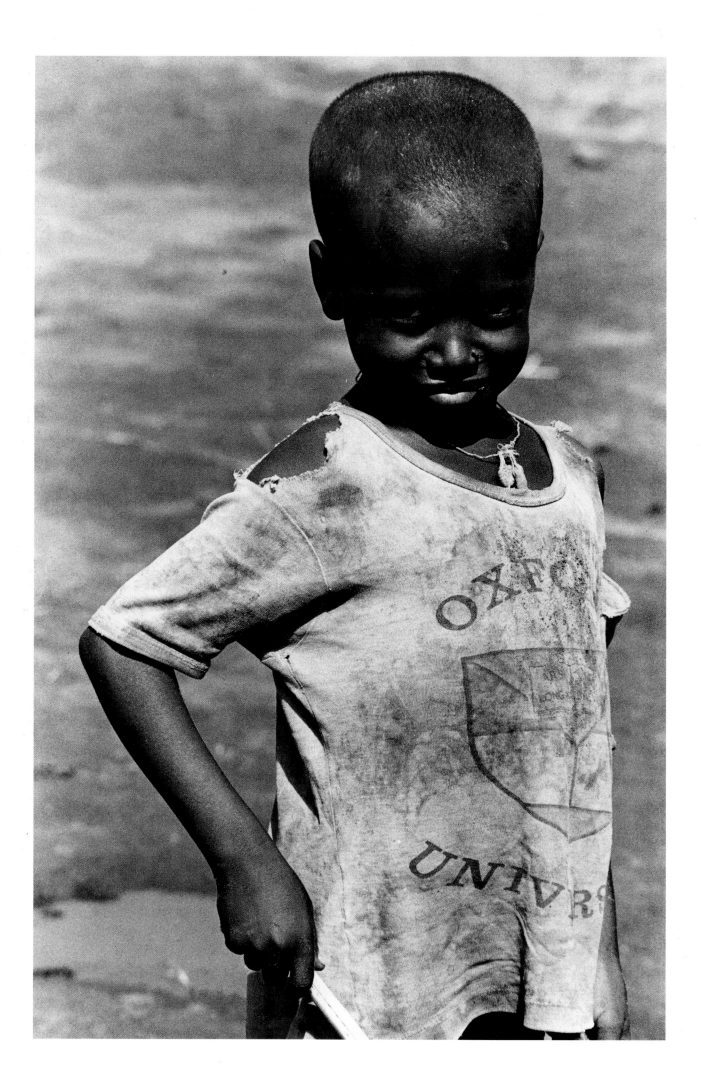

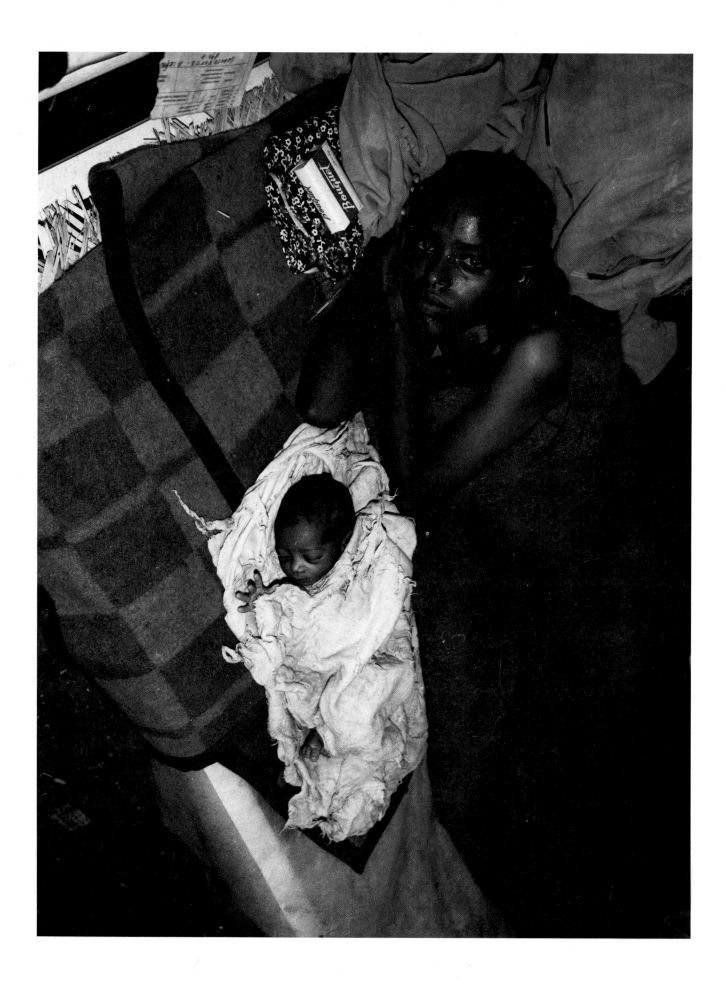

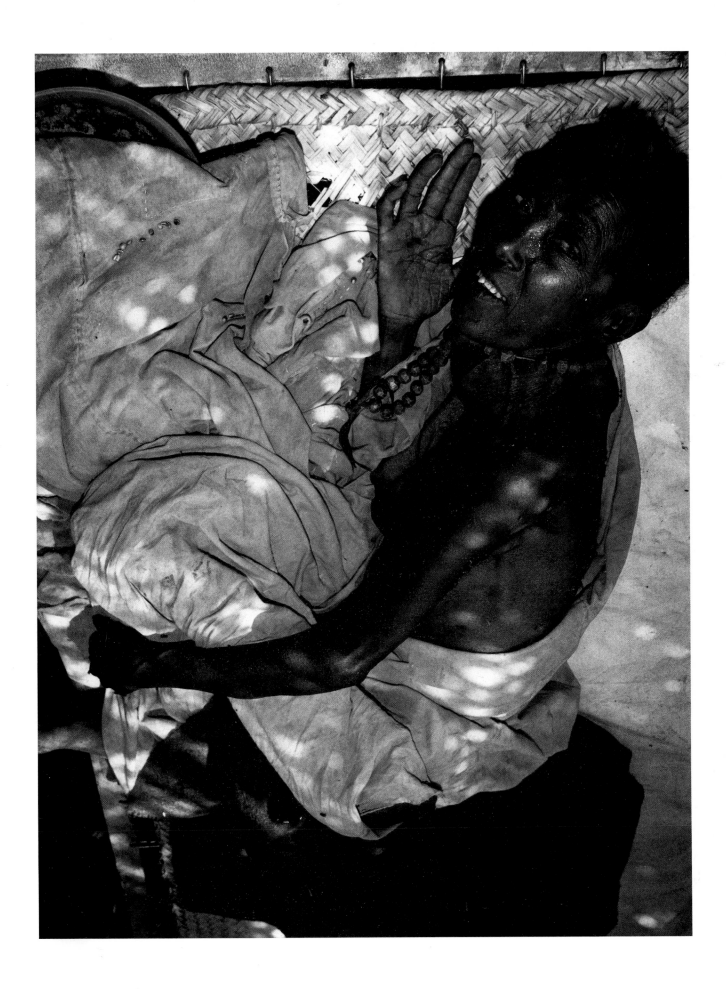

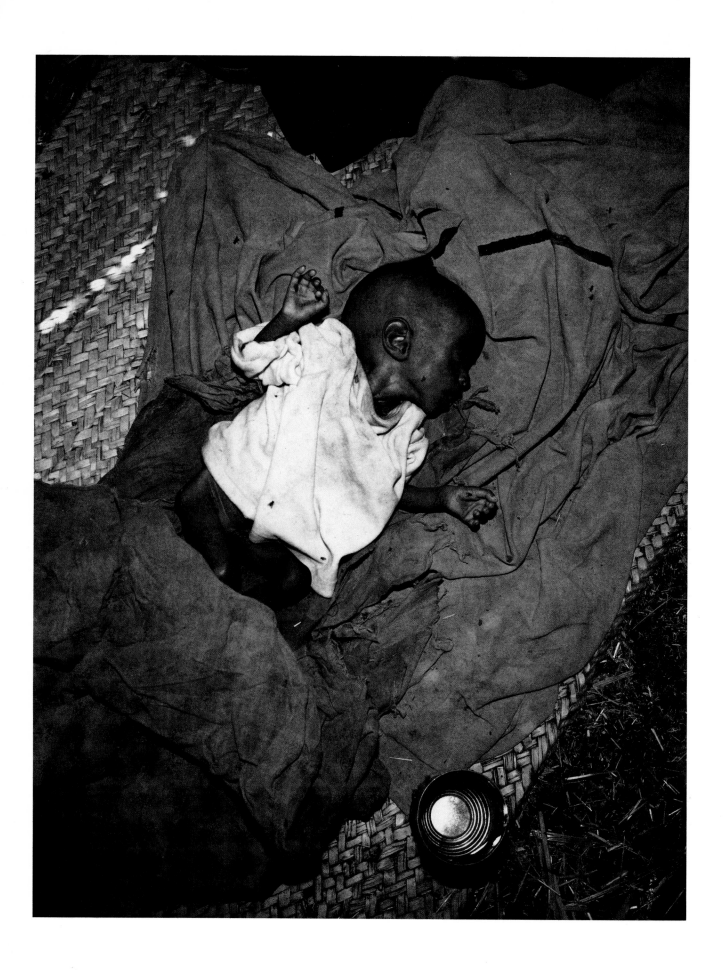

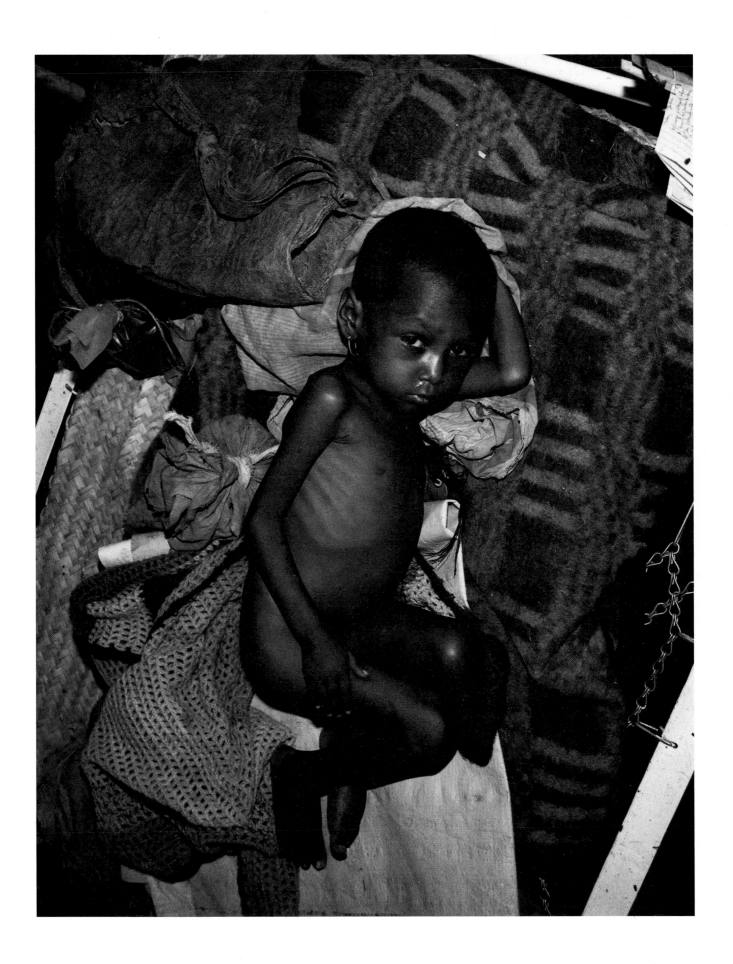

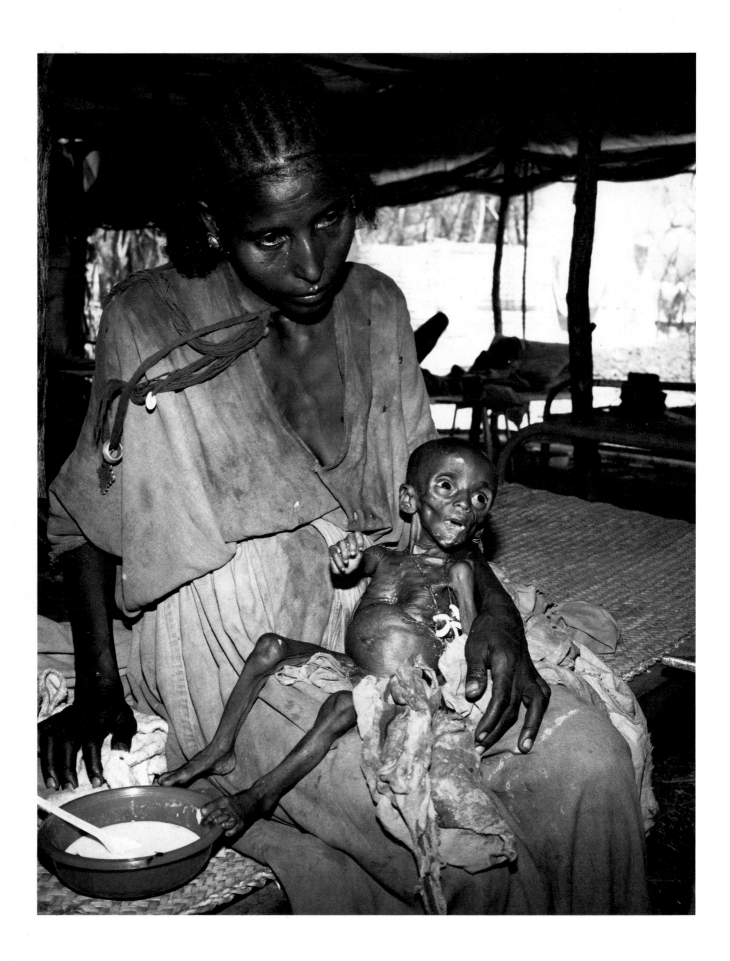

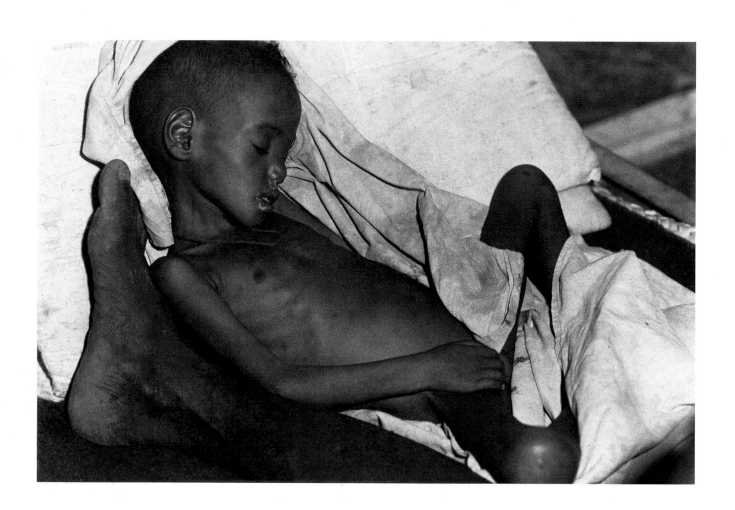

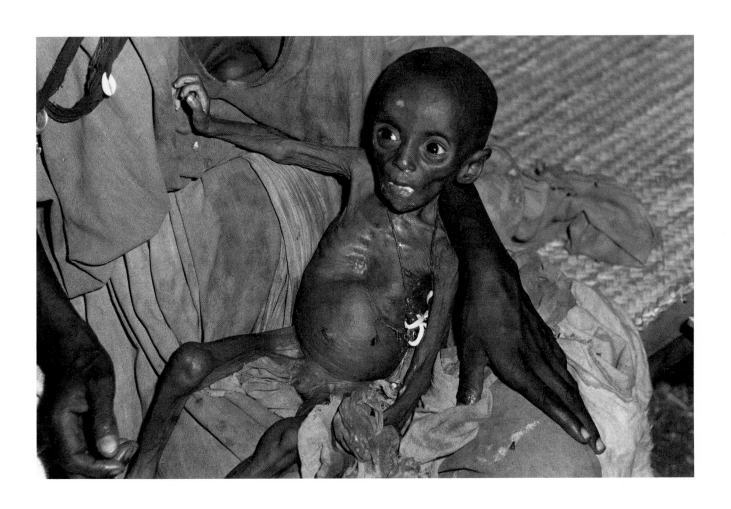

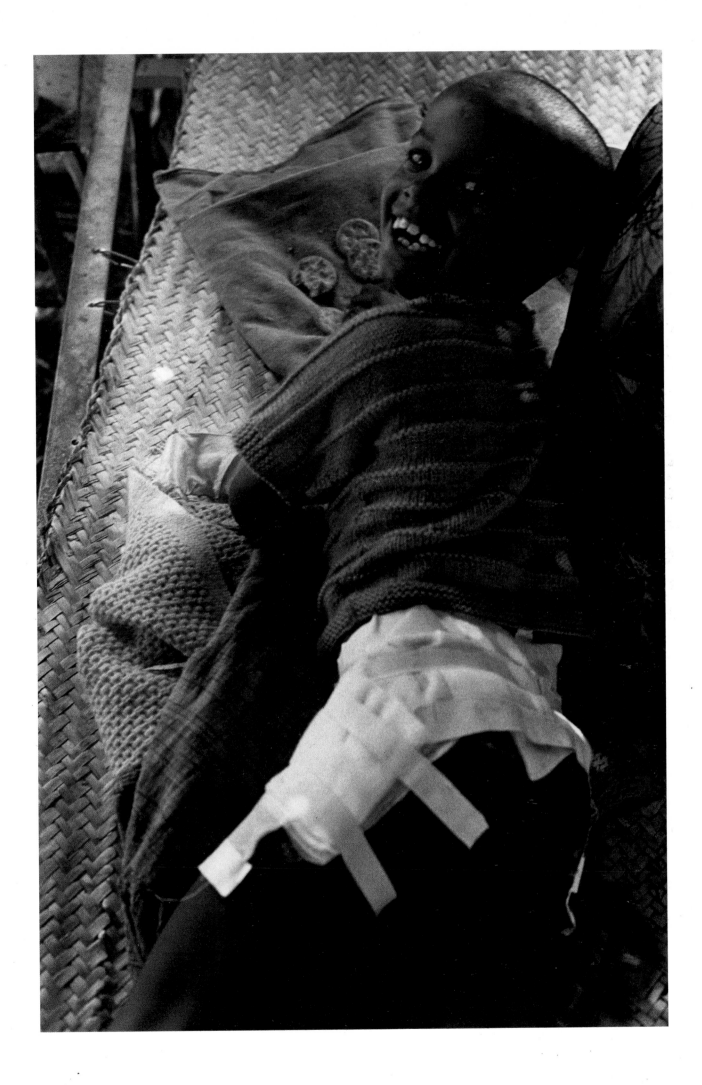

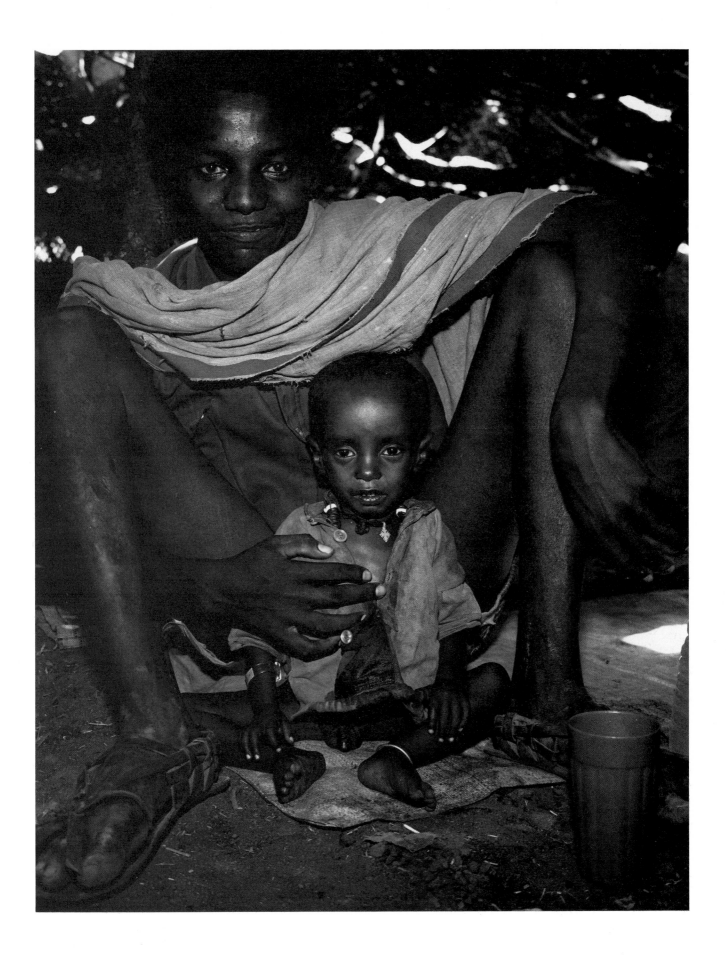

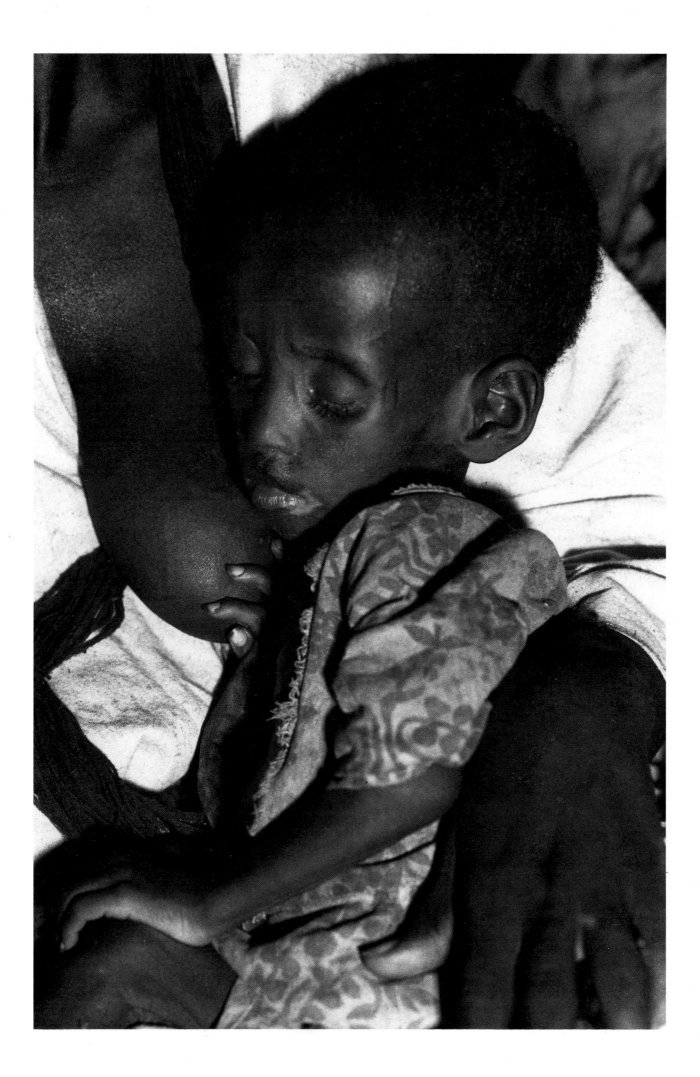

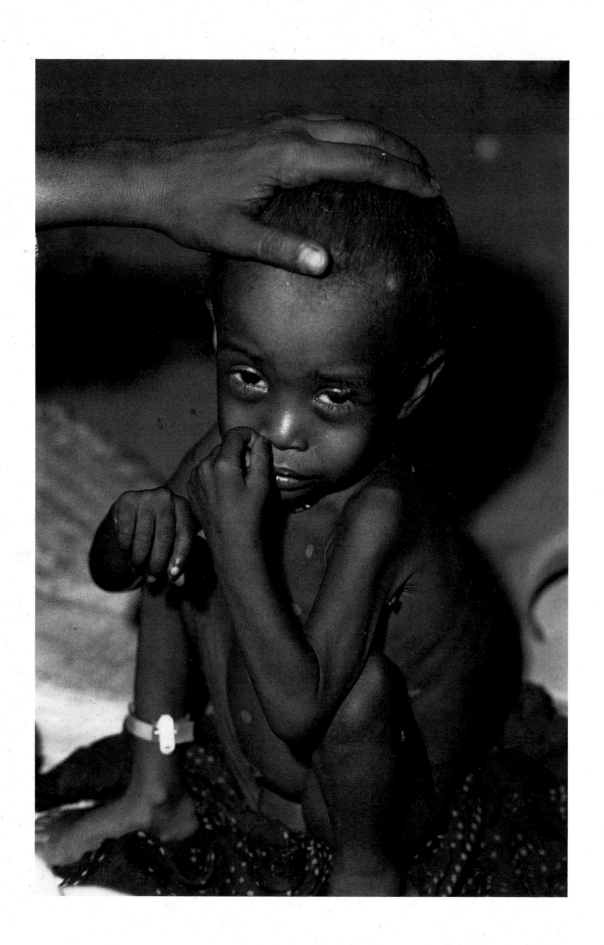

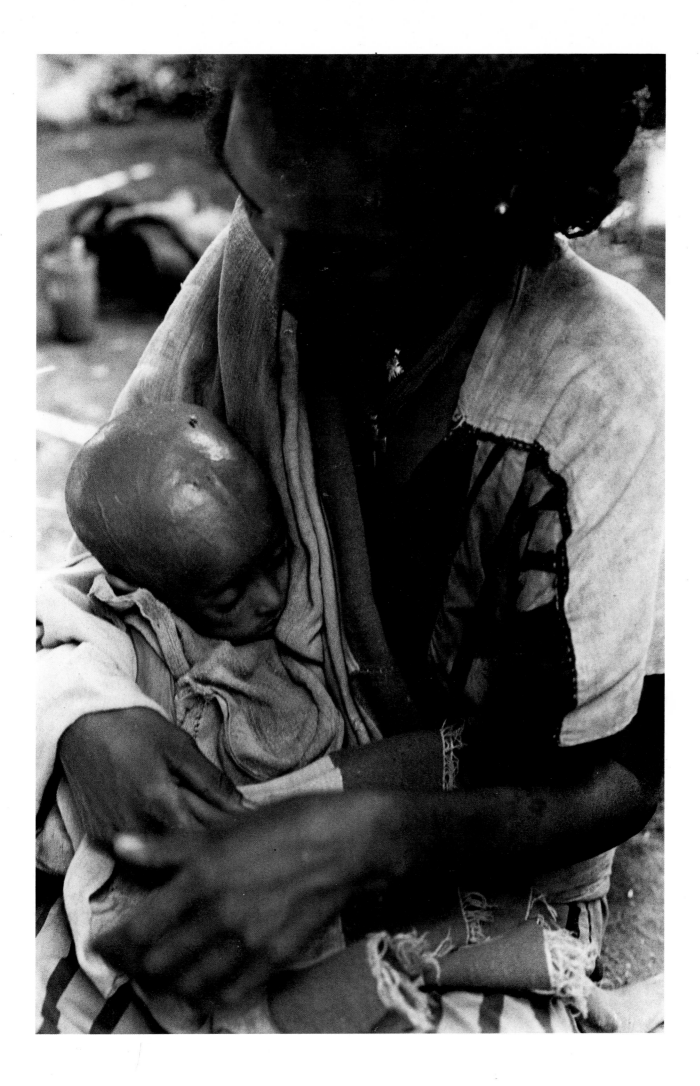

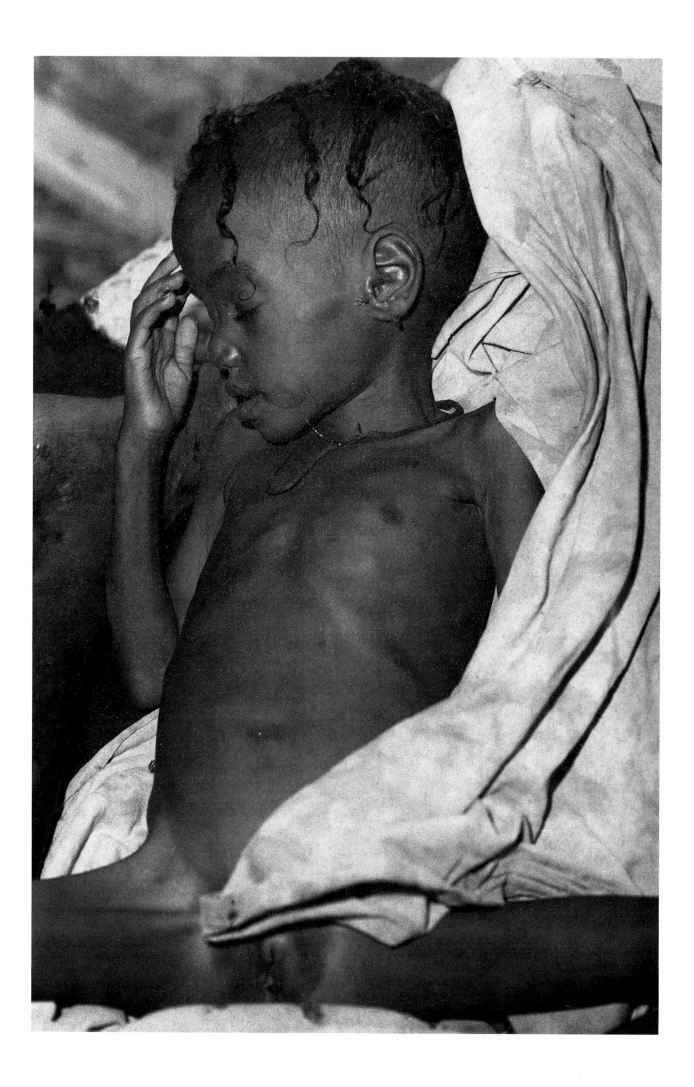

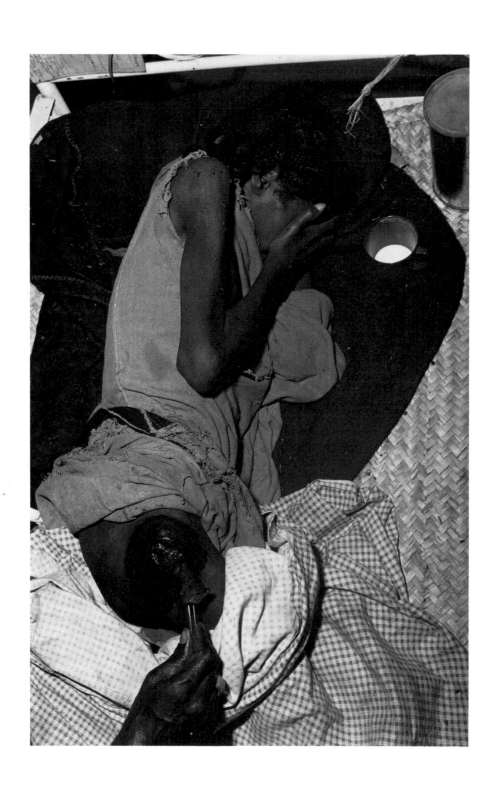

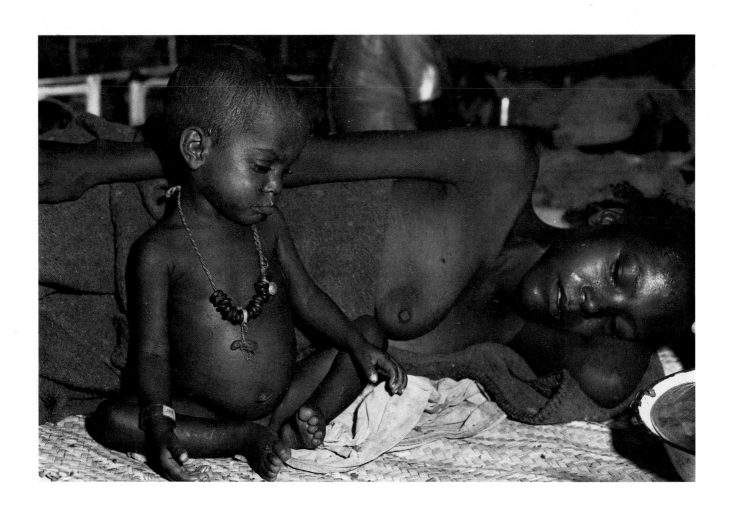

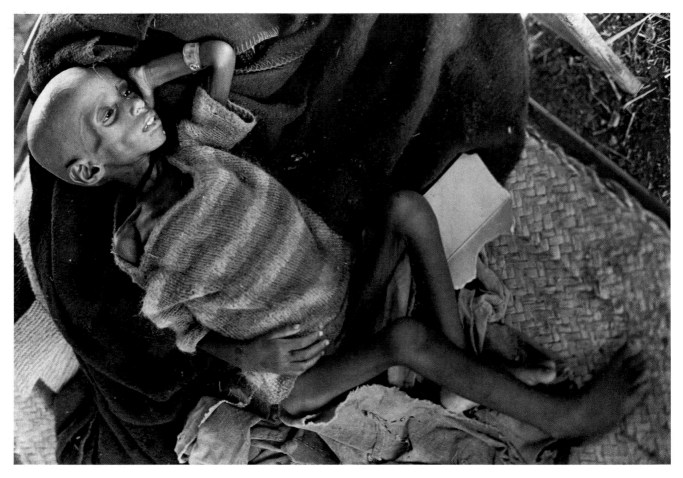

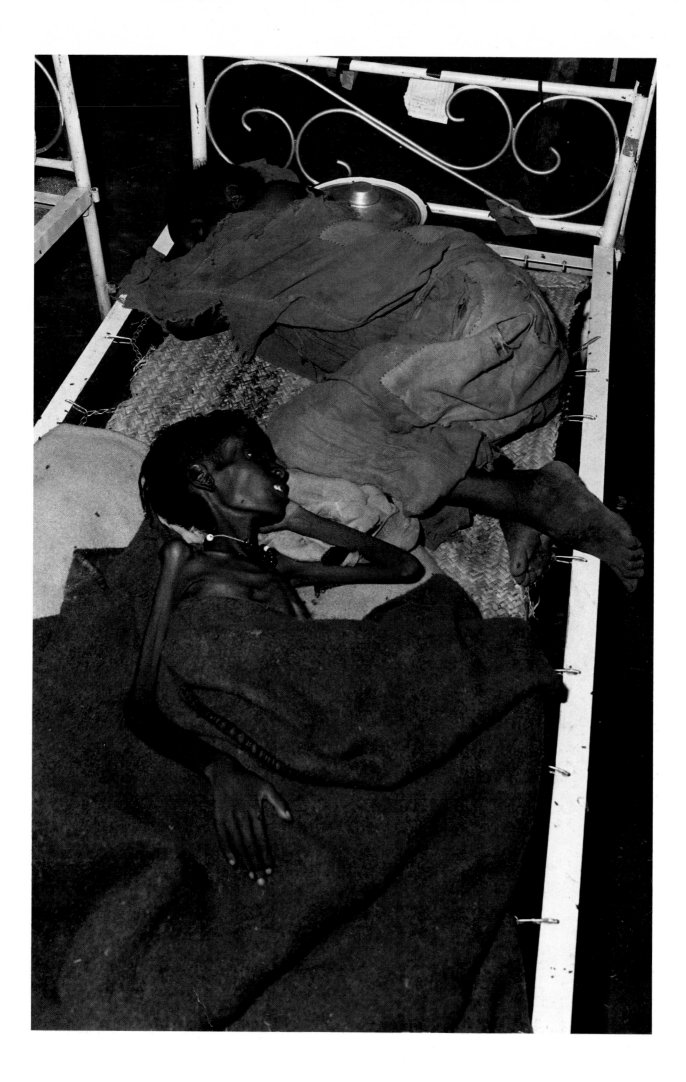

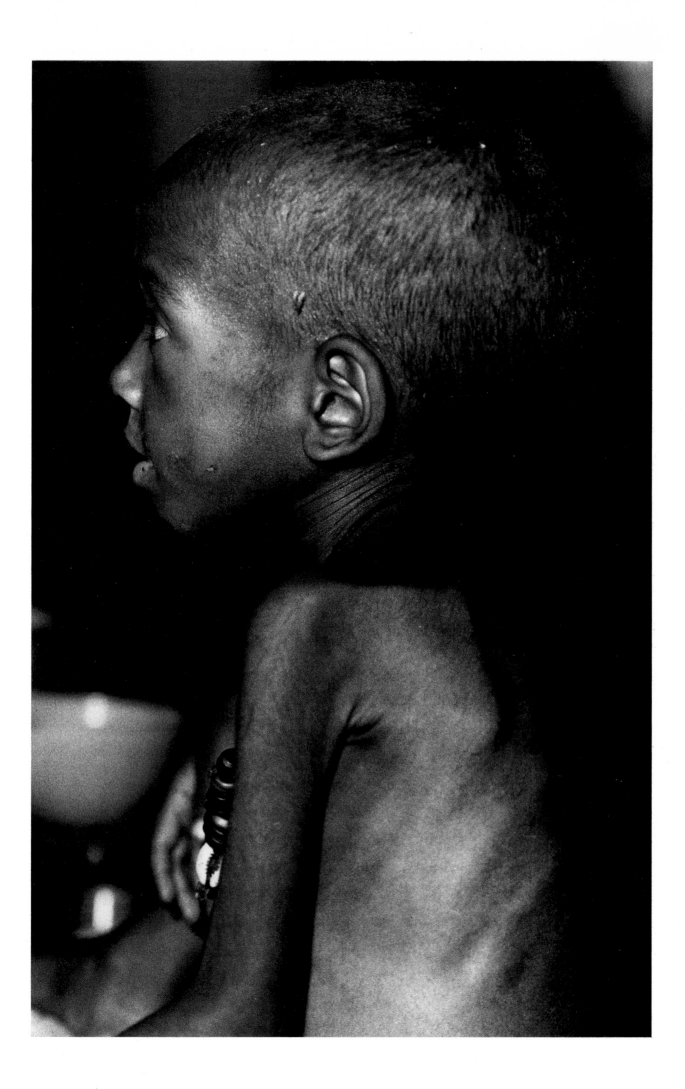

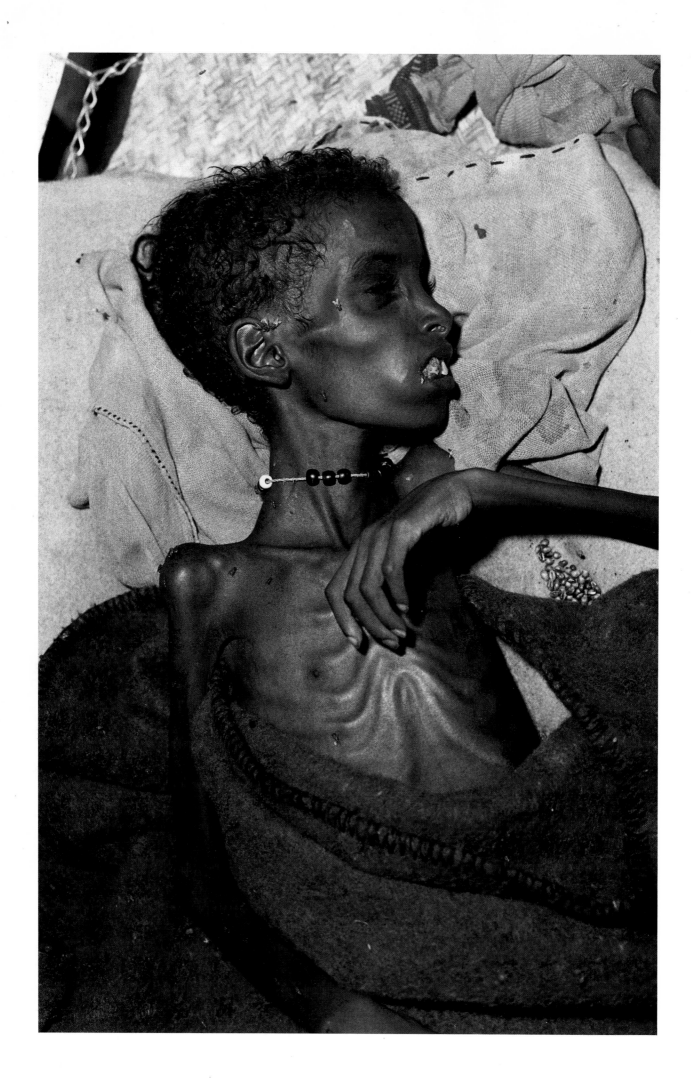

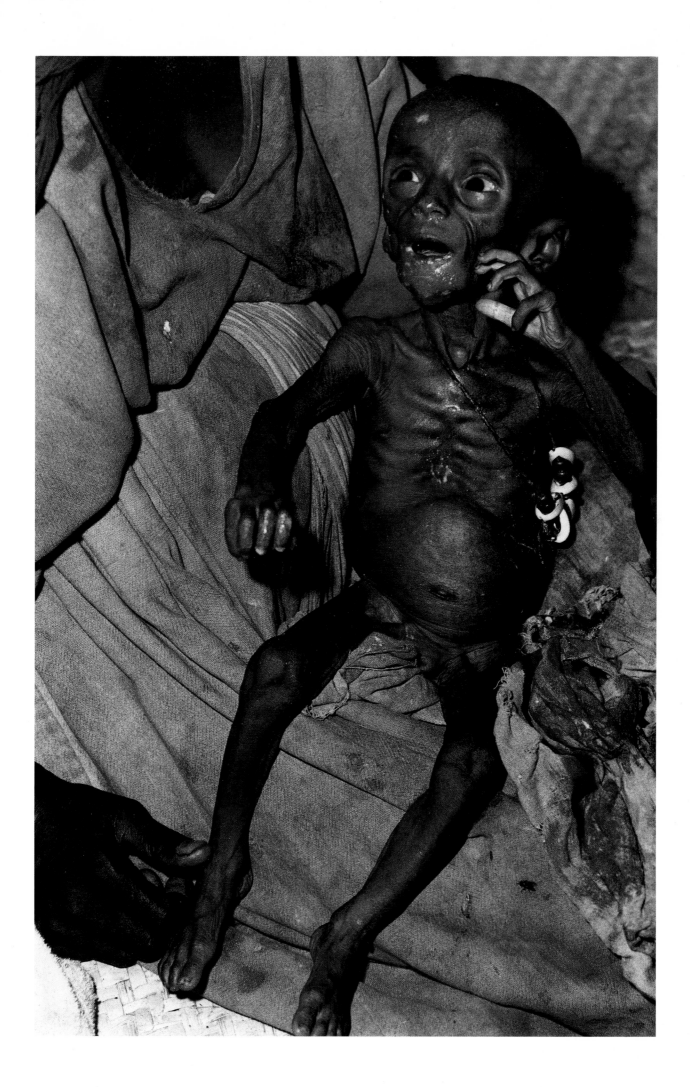

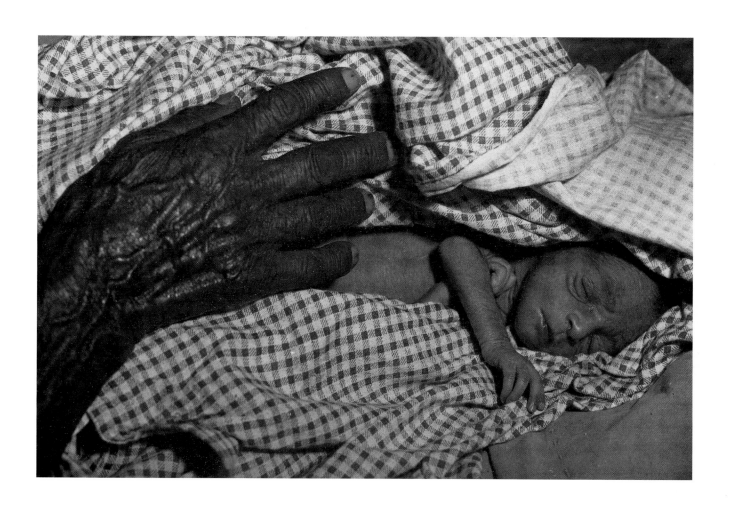